The Nature Kid's Guide to
EAGLES

DAVID ANDERSON

LP Media Inc. Publishing
Text copyright © 2026 by LP Media Inc.
All rights reserved.

For information address LP Media Inc. Publishing,
30012 Variolite St NW, Princeton MN 55371
www.lpmedia.org

Publication Data

Eagles
The Nature Kid's Guide to Eagles — First edition.

Summary: "Learn all about Eagles, the Nature Kid Way"
— Provided by publisher.

ISBN: 979-8-89818-193-2

[1. Eagles – Non-Fiction] I. Title.

Title: The Nature Kid's Guide to Eagles

CONTENTS

APEX AVIATORS

Eagles can spot a rabbit from two miles away! That's like seeing a penny on the ground from the top of a skyscraper!

Whoosh! A bald eagle soars low above a shiny lake.

Eagles live all over the world, from tall mountains to deep forests to rushing rivers.

There are over 60 different species, and they come in many sizes. But they all share one thing: they are born to hunt.

Eagles belong to a group of hunters called **raptors**. They soar high on wide wings, scanning the ground far below. When they spot a meal, they fold their wings and dive. Some eagles can reach speeds of 150 miles per hour on the way down. No wonder they are called kings of the sky!

RAPTOR REVEALED
FUN FACT!
A golden eagle can squeeze its talons with 750 pounds of force — ten times harder than a human grip!

Crunch! A golden eagle tears meat with its curved beak.

An eagle's body is built for one thing — hunting. Its curved beak is razor sharp, able to rip through tough meat with ease. Strong legs end in massive talons that clamp down on **prey** like a vice and do not let go.

Eagles also have hollow bones, making them much lighter than they look. A bald eagle's entire skeleton weighs only about half a pound — less than a can of soup!

Thick feathers cover an eagle from head to tail, blocking rain and keeping the bird warm in icy winds. An eagle has over 7,000 feathers on its body, and every single one has a job.

EAGLE EYES

FUN
FACT!

If people had eagle eyes, we
could read a book from across a
football field!

8

Freeze! A harpy eagle locks its sharp eyes on the dark jungle below.

Eagles have the best eyes of any bird. They can see four to five times better than we can! A rabbit hiding in tall grass is easy for an eagle to spot.

Each eye has a special part for seeing far away and another part for seeing up close. This lets eagles zoom in like a camera. They can also see sideways and forward at the same time.

Eagles can see more colors than people can, including ultraviolet light. That is how they find prey from way up in the sky.

THERMAL TITANS

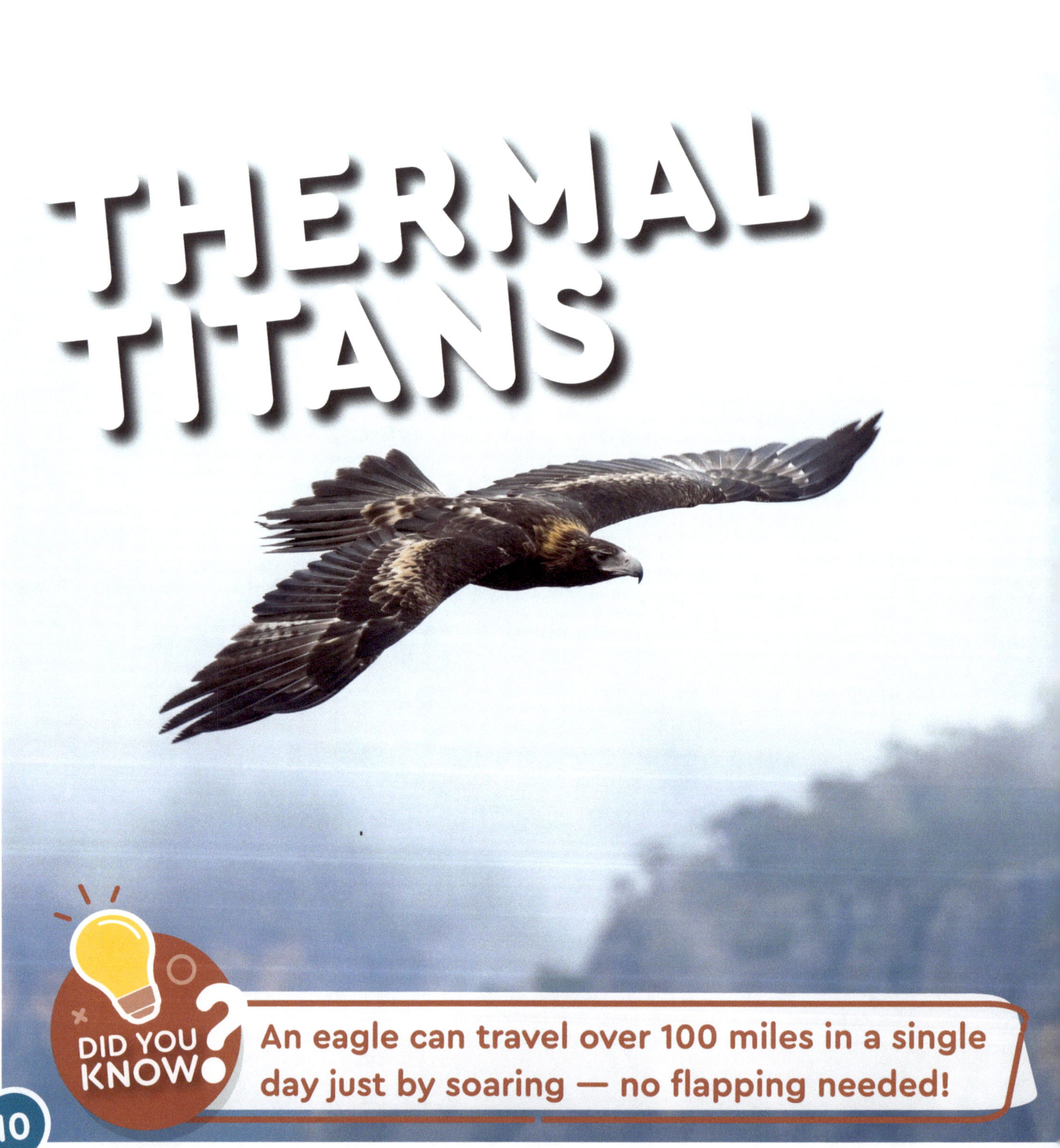

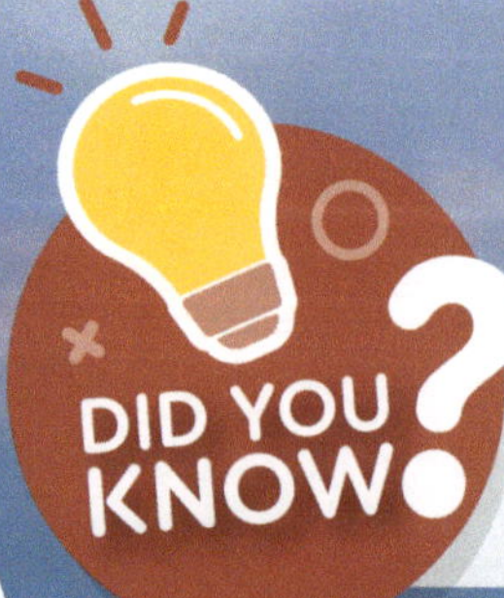

DID YOU KNOW? An eagle can travel over 100 miles in a single day just by soaring — no flapping needed!

Swoosh! A wedge-tailed eagle rides a warm gust into the clouds.

Eagles are masters of the sky. They ride pockets of rising warm air called **thermals**, which lift them high without a single flap of their wings.

Wide wings help eagles glide for miles, tilting and leaning to steer through the wind. Some eagles can stay in the air for hours without getting tired.

When it is time to go fast, an eagle tucks its wings tight against its body and dives like a rocket. This dive is called a stoop — and it builds up so much speed that prey on the ground has almost no time to escape.

TALON TACTICS

Swoop! A golden eagle dives toward a rabbit on the ground.

Eagles hunt in many clever ways. Some soar high, then dive at top speed. Others glide low over fields to surprise their prey.

Most eagles eat fish, birds, or small animals. They grab prey with their strong **talons** and carry it to a safe spot to eat. A bald eagle can lift and fly off with prey up to 4 pounds — nearly 40% of its own body weight!

Some eagles hunt together as a pair. One scares the prey out of hiding. The other flies in for the catch. Teamwork makes hunting easier.

The biggest eagle nest ever found was 9 feet wide and 20 feet deep — taller than a giraffe!

Watch! A pair of eagles surveys the misty valley from their nest.

Eagle pairs build huge nests from sticks and grass. They add more each year, so nests can grow very big. Some bald eagle nests weigh as much as a small car!

The mother lays one to three eggs. Both parents take turns keeping the eggs warm. In about five to seven weeks, the chicks hatch.

Baby eagles are called **eaglets**. They have soft white fluff at first. Their parents bring them food until they learn to fly, which takes about 12 weeks.

SOARING SYMBOL

Over 25 countries have an eagle on their coat of arms or flag: more than any other bird!

Flap! An bald eagle lifts off and soars over an old stone castle.

People have loved eagles for thousands of years. Their size, power, and fierce eyes made them a symbol of strength and freedom. You can find eagles on flags, coins, and stamps all around the world.

The bald eagle became the national bird of the United States in 1782. It was picked because it is found only in North America and looks bold and free.

Even the ancient Romans carried golden eagle symbols called standards into battle. Eagles have stood for bravery and strength for a very long time, and they still do today.

BALD BRILLIANCE

FUN FACT!
Young bald eagles have brown heads — they don't get their famous white feathers until age five!

Splash! A bald eagle swoops and grabs at a fish. It missed!

Bald eagles are not really bald! Their name comes from an old word that means white. Adults have bright white heads and dark brown bodies.

These big birds live near lakes and rivers in North America. They eat mostly fish. They dive down and snatch fish with their talons, sometimes grabbing them right off the water's surface.

Long ago, a harmful spray called DDT made their eggs too thin to hatch. People stopped using it, and bald eagles came back strong! Today there are over 300,000 bald eagles in North America.

GOLDEN GLIDERS
DID YOU KNOW?
A golden eagle can dive at over 150 miles per hour. That's as fast as a race car!
20

Swish! A golden eagle swoops over a rocky mountain ridge.

Golden eagles get their name from the gold feathers on their necks. The rest of their body is dark brown. They are big, strong birds with wingspans up to 7 feet wide.

These eagles live in open hills and mountains. You can find them in North America, Europe, and Asia. They hunt rabbits, squirrels, and even foxes.

Golden eagles drop down fast to grab prey. They are very brave! They will try to catch animals much bigger than they are, including deer and even young wolves!

HARPY HUNTER

Snap! A harpy eagle spots a monkey on a tree branch. It dives in!

Harpy eagles are some of the biggest eagles in the world. They live in the rain forests of Central and South America. Their legs are as thick as your wrist!

These powerful eagles hunt monkeys and sloths high up in the trees. They weave between branches at full speed with remarkable skill, making the dense jungle canopy feel like an open highway.

Harpy eagles have gray and white feathers and a striking crown of feathers on their heads that fans out when they are excited or angry. It makes them look like they mean business!

PHILIPPINE PRIDE
DID YOU KNOW?
Killing a Philippine eagle is a crime — the punishment is 12 years in jail!
24

Screech! A Philippine eagle calls from a tall forest tree.

The Philippine eagle is one of the rarest eagles on Earth. It lives only on a few islands in the Philippines. It is also one of the tallest eagles in the world, standing over 3 feet tall!

This eagle has shaggy brown feathers on its head like a lion's mane. It hunts monkeys, flying lemurs, and large bats in the thick forest.

Sadly, fewer than 800 of these eagles are left in the wild. People are cutting down the forests where they live. But there is hope. Many groups are working hard to save them before it is too late.

WEDGE-TAIL WARRIORS

Wedge-tailed eagles will even attack drones and model planes that fly into their territory!

Screech! A wedge-tailed eagle circles high above the outback.

The wedge-tailed eagle is the biggest hunting bird in Australia. Its tail comes to a point like a wedge. Its wings can stretch over 7 feet wide!

These eagles live in deserts, forests, and open plains. They eat rabbits, lizards, and snakes. They may even hunt young kangaroos!

Wedge-tailed eagles love to soar. They ride thermals higher than most other eagles. People have spotted them flying at 11,000 feet — that's higher up than some small planes fly!

YELPING ROYALTY

The African fish eagle is the national bird of four different countries!

28

Yelp! An African fish eagle calls across a wide lake.

The African fish eagle has a loud, ringing call. Many people say it is the voice of Africa. You can hear it ring out over lakes and rivers for miles.

This eagle has a white head and chest with brown wings. It looks a lot like the bald eagle! It snatches fish from the water with its rough, bumpy feet that grip slippery scales.

African fish eagles live near water in sub-Saharan Africa. They perch on tall trees and watch for fish to swim close to the surface. When they spot one, they swoop down in seconds.

MARTIAL MIGHT

A martial eagle can knock down an animal four times its own weight — like a kid tackling a grown-up!

Thud! A martial eagle swoops down towards its prey.

The martial eagle is the largest eagle in Africa. It has dark feathers on top and a white belly with brown spots. Its eyes are bright yellow and very sharp.

Martial eagles hunt from high in the sky. They dive down fast to catch hares, big birds, lizards, and even small antelopes. They are one of the strongest eagles on Earth!

These eagles need lots of space to hunt. Each pair roams an area of up to 400 square miles. Sadly, their numbers are going down as people take over their land.

SERPENT STRIKER

Hiss! A crested serpent eagle drops on a snake in the grass.

Crested serpent eagles love to eat snakes. They sit on a branch and watch the ground below. When a snake slides by, the eagle drops down to grab it.

These eagles live in the forests of Asia. They have brown feathers and a black and white crest on their heads. Their short, round wings help them fly through thick trees.

Crested serpent eagles have thick scales on their legs. This armor helps keep them safe from snake bites, even from deadly cobras and vipers!

EAGLE EXTREMES

The smallest eagle is the Great Nicobar serpent eagle, it weighs just one pound!

Freeze! A Steller's sea eagle rules its frozen shoreline.

Eagles hold some amazing records. The Steller's sea eagle is the heaviest eagle alive. It can weigh up to 20 pounds — about as heavy as some dogs!

Long ago, an even bigger eagle lived in New Zealand. It was called Haast's eagle. It weighed up to 30 pounds and hunted giant flightless birds. Sadly, it went extinct about 600 years ago.

These record-breaking birds can also live surprisingly long lives. Some eagles survive for 30 years or more in the wild. In zoos, a few have lived past the age of 50. That is older than most dogs or cats ever get!

SOARING SURVIVORS
DID YOU KNOW?
The Spanish imperial eagle once dropped to just 30 breeding pairs in the 1960s. Today there are over 800 pairs — one of the greatest eagle recoveries in history!

Crash! Another forest tree falls where eagles make their homes.

Many eagles around the world are in danger. Forests are cut down where eagles nest. Poisons, power lines, and pollution also hurt them.

But there is good news, too! People are working hard to help. Laws now protect many kinds of eagles. Groups raise young eagles and set them free in the wild.

Safe nesting areas have been set aside for eagles. When people work together, eagles can come back strong. The bald eagle went from 400 pairs to over 300,000 birds! Every person can help protect these amazing birds.

EAGLES FLY

FUN FACT!

You can watch live eagle nest cameras online from all over the world — some have millions of viewers!

Whirr! A golden eagle beats its wings and soars into the blue sky.

Eagles have soared over our planet for millions of years. They have watched mountains rise and rivers change. And today, if you know where to look, you can still find them ruling the sky.

You can help make sure eagles are still soaring long after you grow up. Keep wild places clean. Speak up for forests and rivers. Every eagle alive today started as a tiny egg in a giant nest — and every one of them needs a healthy world to fly in.

Look up. Your eagle might be up there right now.

GLOSSARY

raptor
A bird that hunts other animals for food.

talons
Sharp, curved claws on a bird of prey.

thermal
A rising pocket of warm air that lifts birds up.

prey
An animal that is hunted by another animal for food.

eaglet
A baby eagle.